Ruml
    Teaching salaries
    then and now.

FUND FOR ADULT EDUCATION
LIBRARY

Teaching Salaries

Then and Now

by

BEARDSLEY RUML and SIDNEY G. TICKTON

A 50-YEAR COMPARISON

WITH OTHER OCCUPATIONS AND INDUSTRIES

Bulletin No. 1

THE FUND FOR THE ADVANCEMENT OF EDUCATION
655 Madison Avenue • New York 21, New York

THE FUND FOR THE ADVANCEMENT OF EDUCATION *is an independent philanthropic organization established in 1951 by the Ford Foundation to work in the field of formal education.*

Its chief activity has been the support of experimental programs which hold promise of advancing education in American schools and colleges. To date the Fund has been granted approximately $57,000,000 by the Ford Foundation.

First Printing October 1955

Additional copies of Teaching Salaries Then and Now are available from the offices of the Fund for the Advancement of Education, 655 Madison Avenue, New York 21, New York.

THE FUND FOR THE ADVANCEMENT OF EDUCATION

Board of Directors

RALPH J. BUNCHE
Under-Secretary, United Nations

CHARLES D. DICKEY
*Chairman of the Executive Committee,
J. P. Morgan & Company, Inc.*

JAMES H. DOUGLAS, JR.
*Under-Secretary of the Air Force,
Washington, D.C.*

ALVIN C. EURICH
*Vice President, The Fund for the
Advancement of Education*

CLARENCE H. FAUST
*President, The Fund for the
Advancement of Education*

C. SCOTT FLETCHER
President, The Fund for Adult Education

WALTER GIFFORD
*Honorary Chairman, American
Telephone and Telegraph Company*

MRS. DOUGLAS HORTON
*Former President, Wellesley College;
Former Director of the WAVES*

ROY E. LARSEN
President, TIME Inc.

WALTER LIPPMANN
Author and Journalist, Washington, D.C.

RALPH E. MCGILL
Editor, The Atlanta Constitution

PAUL MELLON
President, Old Dominion Foundation

WALTER E. PAEPCKE
*Chairman of the Board,
Container Corporation of America*

Officers

CLARENCE H. FAUST
President

ALVIN C. EURICH
Vice President

PHILIP H. COOMBS
Secretary and Director of Research

JOHN K. WEISS
Assistant Vice President and Treasurer

Executive Staff

JOHN J. SCANLON
Deputy Director of Research

ELIZABETH PASCHAL
Assistant to the President

ARNOLD J. KUESEL
Assistant Treasurer

Table of Contents

	Page
FOREWORD	9
INFERENCES AND IMPRESSIONS	
Purpose and Method	13
Findings	17
The Reasons Why	21
Implications	23
Responsibility	25
TECHNICAL REPORT	
Introduction	29
Analysis for the 50-Year Period 1904-1953	31
Analysis of Trends in Industry and Education	36
Comparison with Earnings by Physicians and Dentists and in Other Occupations 1929-1953	40
Changes in Top Level Salaries in the Field of Education 1908-1953	45
STATISTICAL TABLES	51
STATISTICAL NOTES	82

FOREWORD

Educators and laymen alike recognize that the most critical problem of the schools and colleges is the adequacy of available teaching and administrative personnel. This is not wholly a matter of numbers although the quantitative aspect at times seems uppermost. Unless the quality of people drawn into the teaching profession is maintained and projected on an increasingly higher level, the education of our children is bound to deteriorate. The long-range welfare of our society requires that a reasonable proportion of our ablest young people invest their lives in the development of succeeding generations.

The question facing the schools is how to attract more of the ablest men and women into the profession, how to provide them with the best possible education for the important work they are to do and how to utilize their talents most effectively in the classrooms and laboratories.

With a deep concern for assisting the schools in their efforts to find solutions for this most critical problem, the directors and officers of the Fund for the Advancement of Education decided to conduct over a period of years a comprehensive investigation of the teaching profession. All major aspects of the profession are being analyzed including its attractiveness, the kind of people who enter it, its holding power, the ways in which professional people are utilized and the promising innovations for improving the status and effectiveness of the profession.

One exceedingly important part of the investigation is the economic. Fortunately the Fund was successful in persuading Beardsley Ruml and his associate, Sidney G. Tickton, to study teaching salaries over a period of one-half century. This report summarizes their findings and gives Mr. Ruml's penetrating inferences and impressions. The summary speaks eloquently for itself. It does not attempt to say what teaching salaries should be. It does, however, reveal clearly how these salaries stand today in relation to incomes in other fields. The teaching profession has suffered on a comparative basis over the years—particularly in its top salaries. What this does to able young people is evident in the small and inadequate share of our ablest youth who choose teaching as a career.

As other studies are completed, they will be reported in successive bulletins. This report will amply serve its purpose if it leads to a better understanding of teaching salaries and provokes discussion throughout the country of means for making the teaching profession more attractive.

> ALVIN C. EURICH
> *Vice President*
> *The Fund for the Advancement of Education*

Note: Advance copies of this study were sent to a number of persons for comment and criticism. Their suggestions have been helpful in the preparation of the text of this study, and a number of footnotes have been inserted to give the substance of certain of the comments.

Inferences and Impressions

INFERENCES AND IMPRESSIONS

by

Beardsley Ruml

I

Purpose and Method

1. The purpose of this study is to examine and to interpret available statistical information bearing on the changes in the economic status of the teaching profession that have occurred in this country over a period of years and to compare these changes with those in other professions and occupations. In this way, we hope to find evidence of both absolute and relative movements of the economic position of teachers at all levels, from grade school through the university, and of educational administrators as well.

2. Only existing statistical material has been studied; no fresh data have been compiled. This constitutes a limitation on the comprehensiveness of this investigation. In spite of this limitation, the quantitative, factual evidence available confirms the impression that over a period of time there has been deterioration in the economic position of teaching in our society.

2A. In some cases the comments go beyond the data, having been suggested by the facts rather than derived from the facts. Clearly in these cases the observations and the experience of others may or may not agree with those of the writer.

3. Two periods have been studied, the fifty year period from 1904* to 1953 and the twenty-five year period from 1929 to 1953. All major classifications of the teaching profession have been included.** Other professions on which there are data of reasonable reliability, physicians and dentists, have been analyzed. Other occupations studied are limited by the availability of statistics, but with one exception, they are believed to be representative of the changes that have occurred. That exception is top business executives, where the only group for which we have found acceptable data is railroad executives. It is our opinion that other top executives have done better relatively than railroad executives, both as to compensation and perquisites, but we have found no data that we felt could be relied upon.

4. On the question of perquisites and fringe benefits,*** there are no adequate data. We feel however that over the years, these perquisites have increased relatively outside the teaching profession and that accordingly the use of compensation figures alone understates rather than distorts the overall impression.

---

*The year 1904 was selected in the first instance simply because it was 50 years before 1953, the most recent year for which good statistical material was available. Having selected 1904 on this purely objective basis, we then took note of the fact that 1904 was not an exceptional year in any way in its own period; that is there were no major wars, no depression, no inflation, no nationwide bank closings and no nationwide strikes. However we do not put forward the year 1904 as a year when the economy was correctly in balance as among its several parts nor as an ideal which we should attempt to reconstruct. All we intend to do is to disclose the absolute and the relative changes in the economic status of the teaching profession over this period. In certain cases 1908 figures have been used because of the availability of statistics for that year which were not compiled for 1904.

**The statistics which are given with respect to colleges and universities are those from publicly supported institutions, since it is only for this group that adequate data are available. There is reason to believe that the salaries paid in colleges and universities publicly supported have advanced more relatively than those of colleges and universities dependent on private support. If this is true, the position of educators in private colleges and universities is less favorable than the figures presented in this report.

***Certain of the comments received stress the numerous and important perquisites and fringe benefits which characterize the teaching profession but these comments do not make a convincing case that these benefits have increased *relatively*. Accordingly they are irrelevant to the point made in this paragraph. On the other hand, one writer points out that the possibilities of legitimate tax avoidance available to those carrying on business activities, such as converting ordinary income to capital gains, the use of stock options and post retirement consulting contracts have worsened the relative position of the teaching profession even beyond that indicated by the evidence presented here.

5. Two observations in general may be made to clarify popular misunderstanding as to the life of the teacher. First, the teacher is thought to gain something in terms of long vacations and, at the higher levels, in the conventional sabbatical year. It should be noted that such provisions have always been characteristic of the teaching profession and that therefore as far as relative change is concerned the vacation question is beside the point. It should also be recognized that such "vacations" are, when properly applied, working periods in which the teacher fits himself through study and reflection for his subsequent teaching duties.* A teacher on a fifty week or even an eleven month teaching year would soon be unfitted for his occupational responsibilities. It is true that many teachers work for money in periods when they are not in residence, but such practices, though they have become financially necessary, are contrary to the educational interests of the community.

6. A second observation relates to a common belief that the teacher gets something more than money out of his work, that a job well done is satisfying beyond the calculus of compensation. This is of course true, but not for teachers only. A good farmer likes to farm, a good doctor likes to doctor, a successful speculator likes to speculate, lawyers like to practice law, transcontinental truck drivers like the power of movement over the face of the earth. Work well done, and suited to the talents of the worker, provided he is not "locked in," as indeed many teachers find themselves — work well done by men and women in all occupations — has a value that goes beyond and is incommensurate with the dollars and cents received in pay. In this the teacher is no favored exception.

7. In order to make comparisons, we have looked not to the

---

*The comment has been made that if the active teaching year were eleven months and the vacation period the conventional three or four weeks common in business that a better case could be made for increased teachers' salaries. In our opinion this would be an error of policy and it would be better to stress the "vacation" period as a working period, at least in part. This point of view should be impressed not only on the public but also on the members of the teaching profession.

number of dollars received, but to the material living that those dollars would buy, after taxes.* Present compensation has been discounted to take account of changes in the cost of living and in the federal income and social security taxes. In order to simplify the tables and the comparisons, the adjustment for federal tax takes the tax situation of a married man with two children. Obviously for the single person, as a result of the splitting of income provisions of the federal income tax law, the reduction in amount of real purchasing power has been much greater — particularly for those in the middle and higher income tax brackets.

8. The cost of living factor probably distorts the relative position of the educational administrator at all levels and of the teacher at the higher levels. This is due to the fact that the cost of living index does not give recogition to the importance of domestic service to the full life of the educator and his family in discharging expected institutional and community extra-curricular activities. No adequate data are available to allow for changes in the costs of domestic service, but it is believed that the use of official cost of living figures understates the overall impression of deterioration, as we have previously observed in the case of perquisites and fringe benefits.

9. Relative changes in economic status within the teaching profession** are as striking as the comparisons with other professions and occupations. The reader is cautioned against any

---

*Comment has been made that comparisons should be made on the basis of income before taxes rather than after taxes on the ground that the money paid in taxes is truly income even though it is devoted to publicly administered benefits which accrue in various degrees of directness to the individual taxpayer. We are of the opinion however that the income that counts for the individual, particularly on a comparative basis, is the income which he may freely use for the goods and services of his own choice. Accordingly in our opinion income after taxes is the best figure to use in making comparisons.

**Several comments were received pointing out that what has happened in the educational profession is a "leveling up" process which has been a general social tendency over the past 50 years. We regard this comment as relevant only to the leveling up process as it affects the very large incomes, incomes which were many times those of the top salaries in the teaching profession either then or now.

mass comparison of teaching as a whole with other work as a whole. For example, over a period of either 50 or 25 years, instructors in large universities have done relatively better than the executive officials of large railroads, and teachers in big city elementary schools have held equal relative economic status with railroad engineers.*

II
Findings

10. *Absolute deterioration.** Taking the teaching profession as a whole there has been little or no *absolute* deterioration except at the top. As a matter of fact, all public school teachers other than those in the big city high schools have gained,** and the big city high school teachers have held their own. Instructors have improved their absolute position and associate and assistant professors have also come out about even.

10A. The serious absolute losses have occurred in the compensation of educational executives at all levels and in that of university teachers of the highest professional rank. Principals of big city high schools show an average drop of thirty percent. The Superintendent of Schools of the City of New York would have to receive $50,400 as against $32,500 in 1953 to restore his ecoonmic status of 1908, when he was paid $10,000. The Commissioner of Education of the State of New York would require

---

*It is important to distinguish between *absolute* and *relative* economic status, particularly when comparisons are made over a considerable period of time. *Absolute* comparisons present the situation then and now in terms of greater or less access to the material standard of living for the particular occupational group under study. *Relative* comparisons disclose how one occupational group has fared, not only absolutely but relative to other occupational groups.

**Note must be taken of the fact that the higher certification requirements for public school teachers and the increased length of the school year have substantially affected the comparability of public school teachers' income over the 50 year period, particularly in the case of the elementary school teachers. There has also been a tendency for an equalization of the salaries paid to women and those paid to men. Furthermore there has been a strong trend toward the equalization of elementary school salaries with those paid in the secondary schools.

$32,250 against the $20,000 he received in 1953 to bring him back to the $7,500 level of 1908.

10B. Top salaries of university presidents in 1908* ranged from $7,000 to $10,000. Today's salaries would have to be from $29,325 to $50,400 merely to restore the 1908 economic position, to say nothing about keeping relative pace with top executives in other lines.

10C. Salaries paid to the most eminent professors also show drastic deterioration. In 1891, the University of Chicago established a rate of $7,000, probably the highest in the country. Today's equivalent would be $38,300. In 1908, top professorial salaries of $5,000 were not uncommon. Today's equivalent, merely to restore the 1908 status, would be $19,200.

11. *Relative deterioration.*** The relative deterioration of education salaries, except for elementary school teachers, is very much worse than the absolute deterioration, and it applies to groups where absolute deterioration has been negligible. Table B, Page 34 shows what would be required to restore relative economic status to four selected education categories. For example, teachers in big city high schools now averaging $5,526 would require an average of $9,400 to give them comparable economic status today with 1904. Principals of high schools in large cities, now averaging $9,156 would require $23,800 to give them the relative economic status they had in 1904.

11A. There are marked contrasts within the teaching profession with the greatest relative deterioration at the top. Elementary

---

*1908 figures are the earliest reliable series available, and are probably about the same as 1904 conditions.

**For the purposes of this study we have used "top railroad employees" as the basis of computing relative economic status. This is a conservative, middle of the road standard, since many occupational groups have done much better than top railroad employees, as Table A shows. However using top railroad employees as our test of relative economic status the coefficient of 60% must be applied to the 1904 salaries, adjusted for cost of living changes, in order to see what present compensation would be required to restore relative economic status of various classifications of the teaching profession to that enjoyed by "top railroad employees." See Table B.

school teachers in big cities have gained 60% in purchasing power in 50 years, instructors in universities 38%. But big city high school principals have lost 30% and university professors 2% which is only an average figure, and badly understates deterioration at the top.

12. Because the greatest deterioration is at the top where the number of indviduals is relatively small, the aggregate amount of money required to correct the situation is substantially less than it would be if the requirement applied straight across the board. The amount required we have not estimated, but it is our opinion that it is not unmanageable.

13. However, as far as individuals are concerned, the increases indicated would be very large indeed, and the correction should be made over a period of time and on a merit basis.

14. The deterioration at the top is so great that it affects the attractiveness of the academic career as compared to other professions and occupations.* The ablest young men and women eligible for graduate and professional training are not turning to education as they once did and as the nation's needs require. The graduate schools do not have students in the numbers and the quality that are desirable; and in the academic subjects, scholarships and fellowships are required to lure them in. No such subsidy is required to fill professional schools of medicine and law, and in these schools there is the necessity of selective admission so that the quality of the professions is likely to be maintained.

15. Comparing the 50 year with the 25 year span, there are interesting and important differences in detail, but the broad findings noted above are valid, whichever period is taken. It is of particular importance to note that the erosion which has been

---

*"An industrialist, discussing educators' salaries, remarked: 'When a teacher's income gets up to a point where you will suggest to your boy that he ought to give some thought to teaching as a profession, then we may be approaching the right figure.'" *Readers Digest,* European Edition, September 1955.

Illustrations of Salary Increases Required to Restore Educators to Their Relative Economic Position of 50 Years Ago*

Amount

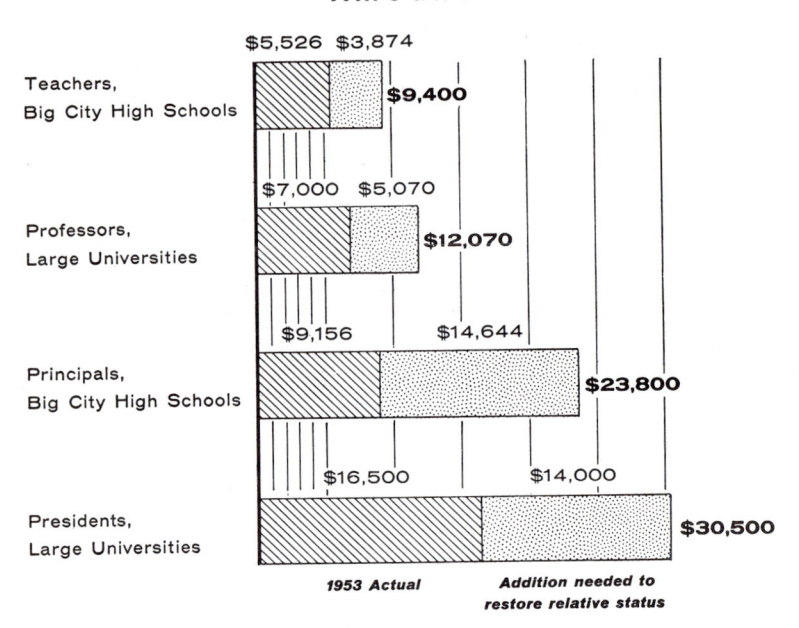

Position	1953 Actual	Addition needed to restore relative status	Total
Teachers, Big City High Schools	$5,526	$3,874	$9,400
Professors, Large Universities	$7,000	$5,070	$12,070
Principals, Big City High Schools	$9,156	$14,644	$23,800
Presidents, Large Universities	$16,500	$14,000	$30,500

Per Cent Increase Required

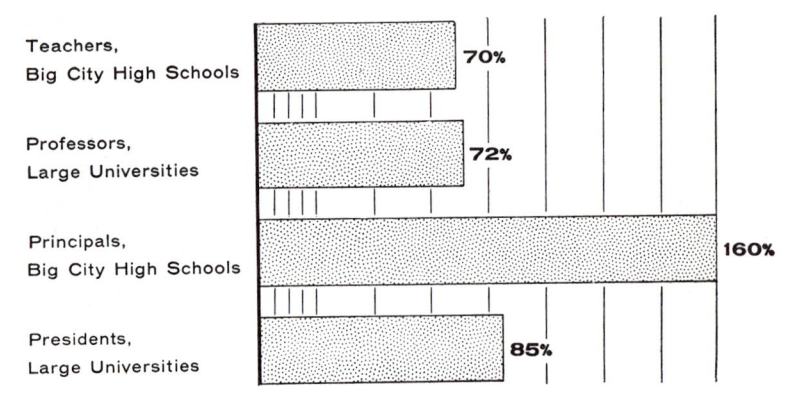

Teachers, Big City High Schools	70%
Professors, Large Universities	72%
Principals, Big City High Schools	160%
Presidents, Large Universities	85%

*Based on comparison of average salaries of top positions in education and in railroad industry, 1904 and 1953. See Table B, Page 34.

observed at the top has been greater in the last 25 years, which indicates an acceleration of the trend observed for the 50 year period.

III

The Reasons Why

16. The superior relative position of the lower income groups of the teaching profession is due to several factors.

17. Increased costs of living made it necessary to apply any available increased income in large measure for the benefit of those who were in affirmative distress.

18. The turnover is greatest in the lower income groups and accordingly compensation had to be revised upward from year to year in order to attract new personnel to take the place of those who were leaving. In attracting new personnel, prevailing markets had to be met. On the other hand, the older and higher paid teachers had nowhere to go. So they stayed on where they were, teaching for whatever was paid to them.

19. The increasing student population created a demand for new teachers and new instructors. But this demand did not require new professors or new school administrators. Such additional income available to education went to meet the market at the lower levels. Higher salary schedules were also made necessary because of the increased length of the school year and because of increased requirements for preparation and for certification.

20. As the compensation at the higher levels of teaching in colleges and universities deteriorated, additional emphasis was placed on security. In many institutions, permanent tenure was given instead of additional compensation. And with tenure came lack of flexibility of faculty appointments. As a result courses and departmental offerings became entrenched, and the urge for

justifying the security of tenure expressed itself in the proliferation of courses and in many cases wanton reduction in the average student-teacher ratio. Educational administration, especially in the universities and colleges, lost control of the faculty and the faculty lost control of the curriculum. Increases of tuitions therefore were not available as they might have been for the increase in rates of compensation.

21. The public schools being tied to the property tax as their principal source of revenue found themselves unable to share in the rising national income, access to which is through the income tax. It is true that the states made use of both the income tax and the sales tax to obtain funds for allocation to education. But because of the competitive position of state with state and the low potential of both income and sales taxes in many states this source of revenue although important has fallen far short of meeting the financial problems of the schools. As a result, public education broadly speaking has failed to participate in national prosperity, and this at a time when the pressures, both quantitative and qualitative, are increasing progressively from year to year.

22. Endowed colleges and universities have been unable to increase their endowment income proportionately to their increased demands and increased expense. Sharp increases in income and estate taxes have reduced the capital accumulations from which endowments formerly came. Tax exemptions helpful as they are in increasing current revenues do not create the fortunes which provide capital gifts. The income on endowments has been unfavorably affected through lower yields on bonds, but this has been offset in some measure by shifts in investment portfolios from bonds and mortgages into equities.

23. The high tax on corporate profits cannot be compensated for in a tax free institution. The vice president of a company gets a salary increase of $2,000; this increase is an expense of doing business to his company, and is deductible for tax purposes. Accordingly the federal government pays 52% of the increase, and the owners of the business can give the $2,000 at a cost to them of only $960. In education a $2,000 increase is $2,000 net; there being no federal tax, there is no federal tax subsidy.

24. Greater proportions of budgets are being applied to non-teaching functions. In many cases this expenditure is justified in that it enriches the educational program; and in any case much of it would have been necessary in view of the management requirements of increasing enrollments. However, these non-teaching expenditures will increasingly be required to justify their place in the educational scheme of things, particularly those parts devoted to alumni relations, money raising, publicity and intercollegiate athletics.

25. The deterioration of the economic status at the top is substantially influenced by what may be termed political or public relations considerations. When there is less than enough money to go around, it is impossible to raise top salaries in a non-profit institution. It is even difficult to raise new money to give equivalent compensation to top academic personnel as against vice presidents of corporations or junior partners of law offices and brokerage firms. Even Congress took many years to raise the salaries of its own members part way to a level proportionate to an earlier day.

IV

Implications

What does it all mean?

26. The American society is deteriorating in the sector most critical for future progress and well-being. The quality of the future depends on education at all levels, and the quality of education depends on its top leadership. The best talent of the younger generation finds that education is not as highly valued by its seniors as law, medicine, advertising, or many technical skills. The response of the talented members of the young generation is rational and what might be expected. The talented members of the younger generation choose to enter law, medicine, advertising, the mechanical vocations, or the arts.

26A. Our society is in a period of rapid change. We face increasing complexities and hazards, both technical and moral. It is imperative that we bring into education a sufficient share of the highest talent of each generation so that each succeeding generation will be the better prepared to deal with the old and new challenges of its own time. Quality in teaching breeds quality in students.

27.* Disaffection is being created at the most sensitive point in our society. We use the word "disaffection" with deliberation. Pervading pessimism, extending in extreme cases to subversion, fellow-travelling, and other educational sabotage springs basically from a sense of unfair treatment by a non-conscious social drift, not from a blazing passion to reform. The pessimism and disaffection expresses itself in lecture, classroom and community activities. And the teacher being literate and articulate attracts

---

*More comments were made on this paragraph than on any other. These comments ranged from enthusiastic approval to vigorous dissent. The observations contained in this paragraph are observations only and in the opinion of the writer are supported by the data although of course they are not derived from the data. The following extracts from the comments seem of special interest:

"This paragraph is particularly significant and will impress many that might otherwise be apathetic."

"Professors who are poisoned are poisoned by the oppressive anti-intellectualism of our society and the consequent status of the academic man . . . the salary is a reflection rather than a cause of the sense of injustice, neglect and humiliation."

"It disturbs me no end to think that the people in the field of education who are presumably at the highest levels of intelligence would have their judgment distorted, even by the facts of injustice, neglect and humiliation . . . some enemy of our educational system might wield this paragraph as a wicked club." "One thing that shocked me a bit in the study is the paragraph on disaffection. I suppose I ought not to be surprised since one would logically expect that result, but it does not correspond with my experience."

Since the paragraph does in fact correspond with the experience of the writer it is included unaltered as it appeared in the original text.

both the other disaffected and the uninformed who earnestly wish for a better world. Adequate compensation is not a bribe nor is it a cure; it is simply an assurance that intellectual leadership maintains a balanced economic status with its contemporaries. On that foundation we can still expect deviation and criticism, but it can be sincere and rational, not poisoned by the facts of injustice, neglect and humiliation.

28. A reorganization of curriculum, facilities and teaching aids at all levels of the educational process is overdue and inevitable — both to reverse the trend to economic deterioration and to meet the requirements of increased enrollments. The situation will be met not with more money only, but with increased efficiency, new ideas on teaching methods, drastic reorganization of the curriculum, and finally a belief in education as a value for its own sake and not as an excuse for a variety of adolescent activities that were formerly carried on without academic sponsorship.

V
Responsibility

29. The evidence, incomplete as it is, points to an erosion of fundamental elements in the American democracy. The responsibility is only partly that of the teacher and the educational administrator. A basic reorientation at the highest level both public and private is required — a reorientation both moral and intellectual.

30. A new approach to the curriculum and to teaching methods is required at all levels. Waste must be eliminated wherever it occurs. Economies can be made that will improve rather than weaken the quality of the educational program.

31. Given a reorientation in which the public can have confidence, the needed resources will inevitably flow, for they are small indeed as compared with the vast and increasing productivity of the American economy. No citizen would suffer any material hardship nor indeed would he be aware of any personal sacrifice.

32. The long fifty year trend can be reversed, and educational leadership restored to the relative economic status and high dignity that were given to it as a matter of course at the beginning of the century.

Technical

Report

TECHNICAL REPORT

Prepared by Sidney G. Tickton

under the direction of Beardsley Ruml

Introduction

For many years, wages and salaries have been rising in all parts of the American economy, but, as everyone knows, salaries in the field of education have lagged in this upward move. However, it has not been shown statistically how great the lag has been, by comparing annual earnings in the various categories of teaching activity and school administration with earnings from other occupations — with all figures adjusted not only for changes in the cost of living, but also to allow for the effect of Federal income and social security taxes. This study assembles such data for the 50 year period 1904-1953, comparing salaries paid in elementary schools, high schools and universities with the compensation received by railroad employees, telephone operators, employees in manufacturing industries, etc. It sets forth a statistical picture of the deterioration, relatively, of the economic position of public school teachers, school administrators, and members of university faculties during the first half of the 20th century as compared with other parts of the economy.

This has been a limited study, however, and has been confined to data readily obtainable. Information in addition to that presented in this report could be acquired; for example, the mass of earnings data accumulated over the years by the Government and by private organizations could be analyzed. Hourly and weekly earnings of people employed as bookbinders, printers, painters, plasterers, carpenters, weavers, loom-tenders, and in a number of other occupations for which data are at hand, could be translated into estimates of annual earnings by studying annual work patterns, analyzing the effect of unemployment on annual earnings during the various years, examining the wage and hour differentials between leading cities, etc. Field surveys could also be undertaken and new tabulations made of data available in corporation and government records. Projects of this nature, while they might provide a better insight into particular sections of the nation's economy, would not change the major conclusions that can be drawn from the statistics already available.

This study includes:

1. An analysis for the 50 year period 1904-1953
2. An analysis for the 25 year period 1929-53, and
3. An analysis of trends for (a) 1904-1933
     (b) 1933-1947
     (c) 1947-1953

The variations in the wage and salary movements over the years are inspected, particularly for the period following World War II when wages and salaries rose substantially and rapidly. Comparisons are made on a gross dollar basis and on a deflated basis — which allows for changes in the income taxes paid by a married person with two children and in the cost of living since 1904.

Because of limitations in the available data, the salary figures are presented on a "cash" basis: that is, they do not include the value of perquisites (such as a dwelling or an automobile provided a university president) or of entertainment or expense accounts, contributions to pension funds, and health or other benefit programs. Some perquisites and retirement or benefit plans existed during the early part of the period studied, but the value has grown, undoubtedly, in recent years.

The study includes also two appendix sections:

(A) A series of statistical tables showing by years since 1904 the salaries or wages received from various occupations and industries on both a gross and deflated basis.

(B) A series of statistical notes which set forth the sources of the figures, their basis of compilation, their limitations, and their comparability, as well as other background material used for the study.

The appendix sections are an integral part of this report. The summary tables appearing in the text refer directly to them and carry, therefore, a minimum number of footnotes, qualifications and source references.

I—*Analysis for the 50 Year Period 1904-1953 as a Whole*

Conclusion: Wages and salaries rose in all parts of the American economy during the 50 year period 1904-1953. Relatively, salaries in the field of education* rose less than salaries in other occupations and industries, with the result that the economic position of people in education has deteriorated over the years, after allowing for income and social security taxes and changes in the cost of living.

---

*The figures in this report are for State universities, land grant colleges and public schools only, except on pages 45-46, where data for the University of Chicago have been added. The public school figures presented are for three population classifications only in order to reduce the amount of detail in the report. These are described as (a) big cities — that is, with a population of over 500,000; (b) small cities — with a population of 30,000 to 100,000; and (c) small towns — with a population of 5,000 to 10,000. An investigation of other population classifications produced results no different from those portrayed by these three groups.

31

1. During the 50 years 1904-1953 wages and salaries increased in all industries and occupations. "Real" wages rose too except at the top of the income scale in the field of education. The figures are compared in the table that follows:

TABLE A

Comparison of Wages and Salaries in Various Occupations and Industries 1904 and 1953

Position	1953 Actual Salary (Average)	1904 Actual Salary (Average)	1953 Salary Deflated to "Real" Purchasing Power*	50 Year Change in "Real" Purchasing Power
Education Position				
Presidents, large universities	$16,500	$4,300	$4,196	— 2%
Professors, large universities	7,000	2,000	1,956	— 2%
Associate professors, large universities	5,600	1,500	1,596	+ 6%
Assistant professors, large universities	4,600	1,300	1,338	+ 3%
Instructors, large universities	3,700	800	1,106	+ 38%
Principals, big city high schools	9,156	3,552	2,497	— 30%
Principals, small city high schools	6,523	1,931	1,833	— 5%
Teachers, big city high schools	5,526	1,597	1,577	— 1%
Teachers, small city high schools	4,292	918	1,259	+ 37%
Teachers, big city elementary schools	4,817	873	1,394	+ 60%**
Teachers, small city elementary schools	3,682	547	1,102	+101%**

TABLE A (*continued*)

Position	1953 Actual Salary (Average)	1904 Actual Salary (Average)	1953 Salary Deflated to "Real" Purchasing Power*	50 Year Change in "Real" Purchasing Power
Teachers, small town elementary schools	3,190	446	977	+119%**
Railroad Position				
Executive officials, large railroads	11,592	2,803	3,109	+ 11%
Railroad engineers	7,352	1,313	2,063	+ 57%
Railroad conductors	6,676	1,116	1,873	+ 68%
Railroad firemen	6,180	736	1,745	+137%
Railroad switchtenders	4,697	583	1,363	+134%
Railroad clerks	3,984	615	1,180	+ 92%
Industry Position				
Workers in automobile manufacturing	4,947	594	1,428	+140%
Workers in bituminous coal mining	4,198	470	1,235	+163%
Workers in electrical machinery manufacturing	4,133	527	1,218	+131%
Workers in stone, clay and glass manufacturing	3,956	527	1,172	+122%
Workers in furniture manufacturing	3,570	452	1,073	+137%
Telephone operators	3,224	468	986	+111%
Workers in tobacco manufacturing	2,709	413	856	+107%

*The 1953 figures are deflated back to 1904 levels of real purchasing power by deducting the amount of Federal income tax and social security tax (where applicable) paid by a married man with 2 children and then applying the change shown by the BLS index of consumer prices. Calculations for the tables that follow have been made in a similar manner. For further details see Appendix B.

**For the country as a whole (including big cities), the average number of school days increased from 147 per year in 1904 to 182 days per year by 1953, an increase of 23%. The increase in small towns and cities was greater. If allowance is made for changes in the number of school days in the year these estimates would be reduced and the resulting percentages may provide a truer picture than the gross percentages of the change that took place in the earning power of teachers during the period. In making comparisons it should be noted also that while the number of hours of work per year by teachers was increasing 1904-1953, the number of hours worked by people in industrial occupations was decreasing significantly.

2. Another way of looking at the relative position of people in the field of education is to estimate what their salaries would have been in 1953 (after allowing for income taxes and changes in the cost of living) if they had done as well as people in industry. Average salaries of top positions in education, for example, would have had to have been much higher to have matched the purchasing power increase (60%) of average salaries of top positions in the railroad industry (executives, engineers, and conductors). The figures are shown in the table that follows:

TABLE B
Estimates of Top Level Average Salaries Required in Education if the Increases since 1904 had been as Great as for Top Level Average Salaries in the Railroad Industry

Item	Presidents Large Universities	Principals Big City High Schools	Professors Large Universities	Teachers Big City High Schools
1. Average salary 1904	$ 4,300	$ 3,552	$ 2,000	$1,597
2. Above amount increased by 210.8% to allow for changes in cost of living 1904-53	13,364	11,040	6,216	4,963
3. Above amount increased by an additional 60% to match top level railroad employees	21,382	17,664	9,946	7,941
4. Amount *before* taxes providing foregoing amount of purchasing power	30,500	23,800	12,070	9,400
5. Actual average salary 1953	16,500	9,156	7,000	5,526
6. Percentage change required to match top level people in the railroad industry	+85%	+160%	+72%	+70%

Note: Tax calculations are for a married person with 2 children as in the previous table.

3. In 1953, a salary of $11,200 provided the same purchasing power to a married person with two children as a $3,000 salary in 1904 — allowing for income taxes and changes in the cost of living. A table comparing the figures for various income levels, 1904 and 1953, follows:

TABLE C

Selected Salary Amounts for 1904 and Income Required to Provide Same Purchasing Power in 1953

1904 Salary	Income Required to Provide Same Purchasing Power in 1953	1904 Salary	Income Required to Provide Same Purchasing Power in 1953
$ 500	$ 1,577	3,400	12,940
600	1,893	3,600	13,815
700	2,209	3,800	14,690
800	2,523	4,000	15,580
900	2,885	4,200	16,520
1,000	3,280	4,400	17,460
1,100	3,675	4,600	18,405
1,200	4,065	4,800	19,345
1,300	4,450	5,000	20,345
1,400	4,840	5,500	22,850
1,500	5,230	6,000	25,490
1,600	5,615	6,500	28,265
1,700	6,005	7,000	31,250
1,800	6,390	7,500	34,540
1,900	6,780	8,000	38,015
2,000	7,170	8,500	41,700
2,100	7,570	9,000	45,660
2,200	7,970	10,000	54,600
2,400	8,770	11,000	63,990
2,600	9,565	12,000	73,595
2,800	10,380	13,000	83,865
3,000	11,200	14,000	95,390
3,200	12,065	15,000	108,210

II—Analysis of Trends in Industry and Education
(a) 1904-1933   (b) 1933-1947   (c) 1947-1953

Conclusion:

(a) Between 1904 and 1933, the "real" purchasing power* of the salaries and wages of most people in industry and education rose substantially, but the rise in the field of education was less, generally, than in industry and the rate of increase was slower.

(b) Between 1933 and 1947, the real purchasing power of a great many people in industry rose further — in some cases a great deal further — but in the field of education, the real purchasing power of people in all types of teaching declined.

(c) Between 1947 and 1953, real purchasing power rose throughout the economy. Many people in the field of education obtained increases comparable to those provided in industry, and teachers in small cities and towns obtained even greater increases. On the other hand, the purchasing power of the salaries of junior members of university faculties increased less, proportionately, than wages in industry.

1. During the thirty years 1904-1933, wages and salaries rose throughout the American economy. "Real" wages rose too, the percentages of increase frequently running above 40% for industrial occupations. A comparison of the changes in the real purchasing power during this period for the various occupations for which data have been gathered, appears in the table on the next page. The table contains also a comparison for the period 1933-1947 and for the period 1947-1953.

---

*Throughout this chapter, the real purchasing power of wages and salaries refers to the annual amount received as compensation reduced by Federal income and social security taxes and deflated to allow for changes in the cost of living. For convenience in presentation and to make comparisons easier, all figures are deflated to 1904 equivalent dollars.

TABLE D

Changes in "Real" Purchasing Power of Salaries and Wages Received in Various Occupations, 1904-1953

Position	Percent Change* 1904-1933	Percent Change* 1933-1947	Percent Change* 1947-1953	Percent Change Net for Entire Period 1904-1953
Education Position				
Presidents, large universities	+ 39	− 35	+ 8	− 2
Professors, large universities	+ 33	− 32	+ 8	− 2
Associate professors, large universities	+ 38	− 27	+ 6	+ 6
Assistant professors, large universities	+ 33	− 28	+ 7	+ 3
Instructors, large universities	+ 58	− 19	+ 7	+ 38
Principals, big city high schools	− 7	− 35	+16	− 30
Principals, small city high schools	+ 34	− 34	+ 8	− 5
Teachers, big city high schools	+ 24	− 28	+10	− 1
Teachers, small city high schools	+ 45	− 23	+23	+ 37
Teachers, big city elementary schools	+ 71**	− 23	+20	+ 60**
Teachers, small city elementary schools	+ 86**	− 14	+27	+101**
Teachers, small town elementary schools	+ 82**	− 8	+31	+119**

(*continued*)

37

TABLE D (*continued*)

Position	Percent Change* 1904-1933	Percent Change* 1933-1947	Percent Change* 1947-1953	Percent Change Net for Entire Period 1904-1953
Railway Position				
Executive officials, large railroads	+ 50	— 29	+ 5	+ 11
Railroad engineers	+ 43	— 3	+14	+ 57
Railroad conductors	+ 55	— 2	+11	+ 68
Railroad firemen	+ 73	+ 16	+18	+137
Railroad switchtenders	+ 69	+ 19	+17	+134
Railroad clerks	+ 47	+ 16	+12	+ 92
Industry Position				
Workers in automobile manufacturing	+ 31	+ 46	+25	+140
Workers in bituminous coal mining	+ 6	+133	+ 6	+163
Workers in electrical machinery manufacturing	+ 52	+ 32	+16	+131
Workers in stone, clay and glass manufacturing	+ 35	+ 39	+18	+122
Workers in furniture manufacturing	+ 33	+ 51	+19	+137
Telephone operators	+100	— 2	+ 8	+111
Workers in tobacco manufacturing	+ 17	+ 54	+15	+107

*For a married person with two children. The percentages cannot be added together because for each period they are calculated on the amount at the beginning of that period.

**These large percentage increases were partly the result of the substantial increase in the number of school days in the year in small cities and towns, as explained in the footnote to Table A. The increase in the number of school days in the year was not an important influence on the percentages after 1933.

2. The figures in the table make it clear that until after World War II, people in industry fared much better than those in the field of education. When the purchasing power of industrial wages in the economy went up, for example (1904-1933), the purchasing power of salaries in the field of education did not rise proportionately. And when the purchasing power of most wages in industry went up again (1933-1947), the purchasing power of salaries in the education field actually declined.

3. In the post war period, the relative performance of salaries and wages for people in industry and education varied. People in some categories of teaching (for example, junior members of university faculties) obtained smaller increases in purchasing power than people in industry. On the other hand, elementary school teachers in small cities and towns obtained greater increases than people in industry. But this was not enough to make up for the lag in the previous four decades.

4. The failure of purchasing power of university faculty and other teaching salaries to keep pace with industrial salaries has been the subject of considerable comment during the past fifty years and there has been a wide variety of explanations. One suggestion has been that low salaries in the teaching field have been due, in part at least, to an oversupply of teachers and potential teachers. Carrying this point of view to its logical conclusion, proportionate increases in teaching salaries and purchasing power will occur only when a shortage of teachers develops (except, of course, for depression periods). These increases could happen locally in particular geographic areas (as well as for the whole country) and may explain, in part, the better showing of teachers' salaries in small cities and towns since the end of the war. During the war, teachers moved out of these cities and towns as opportunities expanded elsewhere, or shifted to occupations in other fields of activity. This reduced the supply of teachers in many areas to a level below that needed to handle the growing student load. The situation has had to be corrected during the past few years by the payment of larger salaries, net, after changes in purchasing power.

III—*Comparison with Earnings by Physicians and Dentists* and in Other Occupations, 1929-1953*

Conclusion:

(a) A 25 year comparison (1929-1953) of the salaries of university presidents and professors and high school principals with net earnings by physicians and dentists (in the absence of a 50 year comparison for which data are not available) provides an additional example of the relative deterioration of the purchasing power provided people in the field of education. Since 1929, the purchasing power of top level education salaries has declined; the purchasing power of the net earnings from medicine and dentistry has increased.

(b) A 25 year comparison of salaries in education and industry, which groups the figures previously used on the same basis as the information on earnings of physicians and dentists, provides a picture of the relative deterioration of education salaries for that period.

---

*Comparisons between salaries in education and earnings in medicine, dentistry and other professions are handicapped by limitations in the available data which prevent direct comparability. Some of the factors involved are earnings outside of the teaching profession, amount of time worked, length of vacations and study time, value of retirement plans, value of perquisites, size of community in which profession is carried on, and average age of the people involved.

1. In 1953, earnings of physicians and dentists averaged $15,000 and $8,500 respectively. These earnings provided more purchasing power — after allowing for Federal income taxes and changes in the cost of living — than did the earnings of people in these professions in 1929, the earliest year for which data are available. On the other hand, the average salaries of people at the top of the income scale in the field of education (whose incomes were comparable to those of physicians and dentists) provided less purchasing power in 1953 than in 1929. The figures are in the table that follows:

TABLE E
Earnings of Physicians and Dentists Compared with Top Level Salaries in Education

Position	Actual 1929	Actual 1953	Deflated to "Real" Purchasing Power* 1929	Deflated to "Real" Purchasing Power* 1953	Change in "Real" Purchasing Power* Since 1929
Physicians	$ 5,224	$15,000	$2,622	$3,888	+48%
Dentists	4,267	8,500	2,142	2,350	+10%
Presidents, large universities	11,000	16,500	5,673	4,196	—26%
Professors, large universities	4,348	7,000	2,183	1,956	—10%
Principals, big city high schools	5,487	9,156	2,761	2,497	— 9%

*The 1929 and 1953 figures are deflated back to 1904 levels of purchasing power in these columns for convenience in comparison with other figures in this report. Using any other year as the base for comparison would provide the same conclusion, but the figures would, of course, be different. Figures are for a married person with two children.

2. Earnings from the practice of medicine and dentistry are more sensitive to fluctuations in the volume of business activity than are salaries at the top level of the income scale in education. Incomes from medicine and dentistry went down as the depression developed (1929-1933) and went up with prosperity — both

in gross dollar amount and in terms of the net purchasing power after income taxes. On the other hand, the purchasing power of salaries at the top of the income scale in education increased during the depression and showed a decrease for the period 1933-1947. In recent years, 1947-1953, the purchasing power obtained by people in medicine and dentistry and the top level in education have been moving parallel to each other, but in no way has education made up for the lag which developed between 1929 and 1947. The figures are in the table that follows:

TABLE F

Changes in "Real" Purchasing Power in Medicine, Dentistry and Education, 1929-1953

Position	Percent Change* 1929-1933	Percent Change* 1933-1947	Percent Change* 1947-1953	Percent Change, Net, for Entire Period 1929-1953
Physicians	—25	+75	+13	+48
Dentists	—32	+54	+ 5	+10
Presidents, large universities	+ 6	—35	+ 8	—26
Professors, large universities	+22	—32	+ 8	—10
Principals, big city high schools	+17	—35	+16	— 9

*Figures on which percentages were calculated were deflated back to 1904 levels of purchasing power for convenience in comparison with other figures in this report. The percentages cannot be added together because for each period they were calculated on the amount at the beginning of the period. Figures are for a married person with two children.

3. The ability of physicians and dentists to do better financially than university presidents or professors over the years is attributed by some observers to the business risks taken by the medical and dental professions. Medicine and dentistry are businesses as well as professions, and the volume of net receipts each

year depends upon the economic condition of the community in which the practice is carried on. Fees can be raised when the community is prosperous; they must be lowered when it is not. On the other hand, education is not conducted as a business, and a large portion of the people in the field are paid by the taxing authorities. Salaries are affected therefore to a lesser degree by business fluctuations or the annual change in prosperity of the local community.

4. Other observers attribute the relatively poor earning position of university personnel since the middle Thirties to an oversupply of Ph.D.'s. They point out that the relatively high purchasing power of people in the field of education during the depression made university employment more attractive than previously; and the lack of employment for young people just out of college encouraged many to continue their graduate work. The proportion taking Ph.D.'s rose nearly one-third, it is reported, and the proportion entering teaching was greater than it otherwise would have been. In addition, starting in 1935 universities added many scholars from European countries to their staffs.

5. A comparison of salaries in education and industry for 1929 and 1953, which groups all figures previously used on the same basis as the information on earnings of physicians and dentists, provides a picture of the relative deterioration of education salaries for that period. Elementary school teachers did better relatively than other teachers during these 25 years because (1) the wartime and postwar competition provided by alternative employment opportunities available to young people just out of teachers colleges forced school boards to raise entrance salaries for elementary teaching; and (2) many school boards adopted uniform salary schedules which brought elementary rates up to those in other parts of the school system. The figures for the various industries and occupations for 1929 and 1953 are in the table that follows:

TABLE G
Twenty-Five Year Comparison (1929-1953) of Changes in "Real" Purchasing Power in Various Occupations

Position	1929 Salary Deflated to "Real" Purchasing Power*	1953 Salary Deflated to "Real" Purchasing Power*	25 Year Change in "Real" Purchasing Power
Education Position			
President, large universities	$5,673	$4,196	—26%
Professors, large universities	2,183	1,956	—10%
Associate Professors, large universities	1,686	1,596	— 5%
Assistant Professors, large universities	1,351	1,338	— 1%
Instructors, large universities	1,006	1,106	+10%
Principals, big city high schools	2,755	2,497	— 9%
Principals, small city high schools	2,105	1,833	—13%
Teachers, big city high schools	1,485	1,577	+ 6%
Teachers, small city high schools	1,064	1,259	+18%
Teachers, big city elementary schools	1,139	1,394	+22%
Teachers, small city elementary schools	807	1,102	+37%
Teachers, small town elementary schools	674	977	+45%
Railway Position			
Executive officials, large railroads	3,734	3,109	—17%
Railroad engineers	1,707	2,063	+21%
Railroad conductors	1,524	1,873	+23%
Railroad firemen	1,258	1,745	+39%
Railroad switchtenders	905	1,363	+51%
Railroad clerks	778	1,180	+52%
Industry Position			
Workers in automobile manufacturing	910	1,428	+57%
Workers in bituminous coal mining	649	1,235	+90%
Workers in electrical machinery manufacturing	831	1,218	+47%
Workers in stone, clay and glass manufacturing	782	1,172	+50%
Workers in furniture manufacturing	702	1,073	+53%
Telephone operators	679	986	+45%
Workers in tobacco manufacturing	491	856	+74%

*The 1929 and 1953 figures are deflated back to 1904 levels of purchasing power in these columns for convenience in comparison with other figures in this report. Using any other year as the base for comparison would provide the same conclusion, but the figures would, of course, be different. Figures are for a married person with two children.

IV—Changes in Top Level Salaries in the Field of Education, 1908-1953

Conclusion: A 45 year* comparison of the salaries of some of the highest paid positions in the field of education shows that the deterioration in purchasing power at top level was greater than that indicated by the average figures for the field of education. Large salary increases would be required to restore purchasing power (after allowing for income and social security taxes and changes in the cost of living) to the 1908 level.

1. In 1908 the salary received by the presidents of the University of California,** Cornell University,** and the University of Illinois** was $10,000. The president of the University of Chicago received $10,000 for the double assignment of President and Head of the Department of Political Science. At the 1953 level of prices, and allowing for changes in the federal income taxes, a salary of $50,400 would have been required to provide a married person with two children with the same purchasing power. Inasmuch as the salaries paid the presidents of these universities in 1953 were much lower than this amount, large increases would have been required to restore purchasing power to the 1908 level.

2. In 1908 the salary of the president of the University of Minnesota was $7,500; of the University of Michigan, $7,000; and of the University of Wisconsin, $7,000. In 1953, about $30,000 would have been required to provide a married person with two children with the same purchasing power. Inasmuch as actual salaries were under $25,000 in 1953, large increases would have been required in these cases too to restore purchasing power to the 1908 level.

---

*The first report on salaries paid in state universities and land grant colleges which provides appropriate data was published by the Bureau (now Office) of Education in 1908. Earlier data, if any were gathered, were not published and are not now readily available.

**These universities paid the highest salaries in 1908 according to the Bureau of Education's report.

3. Figures on 1908 salaries of these university presidents and 1953 equivalents before taxes are shown in the table that follows:

TABLE H
President's Salary in 1908 at Seven Universities and
Amount Necessary to Provide Same "Real" Purchasing Power in 1953

University	Actual Salary Received 1908 (No Income Taxes)	Amount Necessary Before Income Taxes to Provide Same "Real" Purchasing Power in 1953* as in 1908
California	$10,000	$50,400
Cornell	10,000	50,400
Illinois	10,000	50,400
Chicago	10,000	50,400
Minnesota	7,500	32,250
Michigan	7,000	29,325
Wisconsin	7,000	29,325

*Does not include value of perquisites which may be considerable. The 1908 figures excluded perquisites too, but the value has grown undoubtedly in recent years. The 1953 figures are for a married person with two children.

4. In 1891, President Harper of the University of Chicago, after consultation with Mr. John D. Rockefeller and Dr. Frederick Gates, established a salary for professors at the University at the rate of $7,000 a year for the most eminent of the group invited. By 1908, seven professors were receiving the $7,000 a year top rate. Top salaries at other universities were somewhat lower — $5,000 at California and Cornell, for example. In 1953, the equivalent purchasing power would have required a salary of $19,000 to $29,000, as shown in the table that follows:

TABLE I
Professor's Top Salary in 1908 at Three Universities and
Amount Necessary to Provide Same "Real" Purchasing Power in 1953

University	Actual Salary Received 1908 (No Income Taxes)	Amount Necessary Before Income Taxes to Provide Same "Real" Purchasing Power in 1953 as in 1908
Chicago	$7,000*	$29,325*
California	5,000	19,200
Cornell	5,000	19,200

*The 1953 figure equivalent in purchasing power to the $7,000 salary in 1891 would be $38,300. All 1953 figures are for a married person with 2 children.

5. The position involving the greatest administrative responsibility and detail in the field of education is that of the Superintendent of Schools of the City of New York. The Superintendent is now responsible for educating 900,000 children, the administration of a teaching force of 36,000, and the operation of 768 school buildings. In this position too, salary changes have not been sufficient to maintain purchasing power over the past half century. In 1908 the Superintendent's salary was $10,000, equivalent, in terms of purchasing power, to $50,400 in 1953 for a married person with two children. The actual salary paid the Superintendent of Schools in the City of New York in 1953 was $32,500. Further details and figures for the Commissioner of Education of the State of New York are in the table that follows:

TABLE J

Salaries and "Real" Purchasing Power Position of Highest Ranking Education Officials in New York City and New York State, 1908 and 1953

Item	City Superintendent of Schools	State Commissioner of Education
1. Amount of salary received 1908 (No income taxes)	$10,000	$ 7,500
2. Amount necessary before income taxes to provide same "real" purchasing power in 1953* as in 1908	50,400	32,250
3. Actual salary received 1953 before income taxes	32,500	20,000
4. Percent change in salary which would have been required in 1953* to provide same "real" purchasing power as in 1908	+55%	+61%

*Figures are for a married person with 2 children.

Statistical Tables

and Notes

APPENDIX A — STATISTICAL TABLES

Annual Salaries or Wages Received by Persons Employed in the Field of Education and in Industry, Medicine and Dentistry

A. *Education Occupations*

    Universities (mainly land grant)
- (1) President
- (2) Professor
- (3) Associate Professor
- (4) Assistant Professor
- (5) Instructor

    Big City Public Schools (Cities Over 500,000 population)
- (6) High School Principals
- (7) High School Teachers
- (8) Elementary School Teachers

    Small City Public Schools (Cities 30,000 to 100,000 population)
- (9) High School Principals
- (10) High School Teachers
- (11) Elementary School Teachers

    Small Town Public Schools (Cities 5,000 to 10,000 population)
- (12) Elementary School Teachers

B. *Industry Occupations*
- (13) Railroad executive officials

(14) Railroad engineers

(15) Railroad conductors

(16) Railroad firemen

(17) Railroad switchtenders

(18) Railroad clerks

(19) All railroad employees

(20) Telephone operators

(21) Workers in the automobile manufacturing industry

(22) Workers in the furniture manufacturing industry

(23) Workers in the electrical machinery manufacturing industry

(24) Workers in the tobacco manufacturing industry

(25) Workers in the bituminous coal mining industry

(26) Workers in the stone, clay and glass manufacturing industry

(27) All workers in manufacturing industries

C. *Professions*

(28) Physicians
(29) Dentists

Note: Figures in the tables that follow are deflated back to 1904 levels of real purchasing power by deducting the amount of Federal income taxes and social security taxes (where applicable) paid by a married person with two children and then applying the change shown by the BLS index of consumer prices. Further details of the procedure are described in Appendix B — Statistical Notes.

TABLE 1
University Presidents
Annual Salary Received 1904-1953

Year	Average Salary Received	Salary Deflated to "Real" Purchasing Power
1904	$ 4,300	$4,300
1908	—	—
1913	—	—
1916	—	—
1917	—	—
1918	—	—
1919	—	—
1920	—	—
1921	—	—
1922	8,700	4,473
1923	—	—
1924	—	—
1925	10,000	4,907
1926	—	—
1927	—	—
1928	10,500	5,271
1929	11,000	5,673
1930	11,000	5,673
1931	—	—
1932	—	—
1933	9,000	5,992
1934	—	—
1935	—	—
1936	—	—
1937	—	—
1938	10,000	6,105
1939	—	—
1940	10,125	5,978
1941	—	—
1942	10,542	4,674
1943	11,000	4,356
1944	—	—
1945	—	—
1946	—	—
1947	12,500	3,900
1948	13,500	4,148
1949	—	—
1950	14,749	4,465
1951	—	—
1952	16,375	4,201
1953	16,500	4,196

TABLE 2
Professors in Large State Universities
Annual Salary Received 1904-1953

Year	Average Salary Received	Salary Deflated to "Real" Purchasing Power
1904	$ 2,000	$2,000
1908	2,279	2,179
1913	2,463	2,144
1916	2,558	2,021
1917	2,661	1,787
1918	2,677	1,532
1919	2,812	1,399
1920	3,262	1,401
1921	3,616	1,743
1922	3,835	1,972
1923	3,952	1,995
1924	4,009	2,019
1925	—	—
1926	4,112	2,002
1927	4,230	2,098
1928	4,327	2,172
1929	4,348	2,183
1930	4,407	2,273
1931	4,480	2,537
1932	4,505	2,839
1933	4,000	2,663
1934	—	—
1935	3,775	2,367
1936	3,951	2,453
1937	4,166	2,496
1938	4,163	2,542
1939	—	—
1940	4,245	2,575
1941	—	—
1942	4,302	2,057
1943	4,400	1,923
1944	—	—
1945	—	—
1946	—	—
1947	5,300	1,816
1948	5,700	1,869
1949	—	—
1950	6,132	1,985
1951	—	—
1952	6,926	1,953
1953	7,000	1,956

TABLE 3
Associate Professors in Large State Universities
Annual Salary Received 1904-1953

Year	Average Salary Received	Salary Deflated to "Real" Purchasing Power
1904	$ 1,500	$1,500
1908	1,646	1,574
1913	1,763	1,534
1916	1,871	1,478
1917	1,944	1,306
1918	2,012	1,152
1919	2,183	1,086
1920	2,447	1,051
1921	2,744	1,322
1922	3,007	1,546
1923	3,049	1,539
1924	3,084	1,553
1925	—	—
1926	3,160	1,538
1927	3,197	1,586
1928	3,298	1,656
1929	3,359	1,686
1930	3,345	1,725
1931	3,418	1,935
1932	3,379	2,129
1933	3,100	2,064
1934	—	—
1935	2,903	1,820
1936	2,973	1,845
1937	3,144	1,884
1938	3,189	1,947
1939	—	—
1940	3,272	1,991
1941	—	—
1942	3,324	1,638
1943	3,400	1,531
1944	—	—
1945	—	—
1946	—	—
1947	4,300	1,501
1948	4,600	1,534
1949	—	—
1950	4,930	1,622
1951	—	—
1952	5,524	1,588
1953	5,600	1,596

TABLE 4
Assistant Professors in Large State Universities
Annual Salary Received 1904-1953

Year	Average Salary Received	Salary Deflated to "Real" Purchasing Power
1904	$ 1,300	$1,300
1908	1,451	1,387
1913	1,511	1,315
1916	1,619	1,279
1917	1,648	1,107
1918	1,714	981
1919	1,766	879
1920	2,022	868
1921	2,334	1,125
1922	2,484	1,277
1923	2,548	1,286
1924	2,548	1,283
1925	—	—
1926	2,630	1,280
1927	2,675	1,327
1928	2,739	1,375
1929	2,691	1,351
1930	2,775	1,431
1931	2,815	1,594
1932	2,800	1,764
1933	2,600	1,731
1934	—	—
1935	2,449	1,535
1936	2,486	1,543
1937	2,556	1,531
1938	2,592	1,582
1939	—	—
1940	2,605	1,585
1941	—	—
1942	2,645	1,332
1943	2,700	1,251
1944	—	—
1945	—	—
1946	—	—
1947	3,500	1,254
1948	3,800	1,290
1949	—	—
1950	4,085	1,367
1951	—	—
1952	4,573	1,341
1953	4,600	1,338

TABLE 5
Instructors in Large State Universities
Annual Salary Received 1904-1953

Year	Average Salary Received	Salary Deflated to "Real" Purchasing Power
1904	$ 800	$ 800
1908	891	852
1913	1,013	882
1916	1,096	866
1917	1,115	749
1918	1,114	638
1919	1,231	612
1920	1,508	647
1921	1,653	797
1922	1,794	922
1923	1,826	922
1924	1,888	951
1925	—	—
1926	1,924	937
1927	1,908	946
1928	1,952	980
1929	2,003	1,006
1930	1,995	1,029
1931	2,069	1,172
1932	2,005	1,263
1933	1,900	1,265
1934	—	—
1935	1,769	1,109
1936	1,792	1,112
1937	1,842	1,104
1938	1,892	1,155
1939	—	—
1940	1,937	1,179
1941	—	—
1942	1,862	974
1943	1,900	920
1944	—	—
1945	—	—
1946	—	—
1947	2,800	1,030
1948	3,000	1,046
1949	—	—
1950	3,202	1,100
1951	—	—
1952	3,656	1,104
1953	3,700	1,106

TABLE 6
High School Principals (Cities Over 500,000)
Annual Salary Received 1904-1953

Year	Average Salary Received	Salary Deflated to "Real" Purchasing Power
1904	$ 3,552	$3,552
1908	—	—
1913	—	—
1916	—	—
1917	—	—
1918	—	—
1919	—	—
1920	—	—
1921	—	—
1922	—	—
1923	5,000	2,524
1924	—	—
1925	5,585	2,740
1926	—	—
1927	5,665	2,810
1928	—	—
1929	5,487	2,755
1930	—	—
1931	5,674	3,213
1932	—	—
1933	4,970	3,309
1934	—	—
1935	4,776	2,994
1936	—	—
1937	5,149	3,085
1938	—	—
1939	5,550	3,389
1940	—	—
1941	5,412	2,992
1942	—	—
1943	5,820	2,480
1944	—	—
1945	5,794	2,361
1946	—	—
1947	6,396	2,159
1948	—	—
1949	7,321	2,373
1950	—	—
1951	8,107	2,355
1952	—	—
1953	9,156	2,497

TABLE 7
High School Teachers (Cities Over 500,000) Annual Salary Received 1904-1953

Year	Average Salary Received	Salary Deflated to "Real" Purchasing Power
1904	$ 1,597	$1,597
1908	—	—
1913	—	—
1916	—	—
1917	—	—
1918	—	—
1919	—	—
1920	—	—
1921	—	—
1922	—	—
1923	2,893	1,460
1924	—	—
1925	2,789	1,368
1926	—	—
1927	2,868	1,423
1928	—	—
1929	2,958	1,485
1930	—	—
1931	3,061	1,733
1932	—	—
1933	2,981	1,985
1934	—	—
1935	2,788	1,748
1936	—	—
1937	2,937	1,760
1938	—	—
1939	3,109	1,908
1940	—	—
1941	3,106	1,775
1942	—	—
1943	3,205	1,452
1944	—	—
1945	3,499	1,513
1946	—	—
1947	4,047	1,428
1948	—	—
1949	4,689	1,576
1950	—	—
1951	4,947	1,497
1952	—	—
1953	5,526	1,577

TABLE 8
Elementary School Teachers (Cities Over 500,000) Annual Salary Received 1904-1953

Year	Average Salary Received	Salary Deflated to "Real" Purchasing Power
1904	$ 873	$ 873
1908	—	—
1913	—	—
1916	—	—
1917	—	—
1918	—	—
1919	—	—
1920	—	—
1921	—	—
1922	—	—
1923	2,052	1,036
1924	—	—
1925	2,086	1,024
1926	—	—
1927	2,192	1,087
1928	—	—
1929	2,269	1,139
1930	—	—
1931	2,407	1,363
1932	—	—
1933	2,248	1,497
1934	—	—
1935	2,119	1,329
1936	—	—
1937	2,270	1,360
1938	—	—
1939	2,469	1,515
1940	—	—
1941	2,434	1,410
1942	—	—
1943	2,709	1,255
1944	—	—
1945	2,735	1,224
1946	—	—
1947	3,200	1,158
1948	—	—
1949	4,019	1,369
1950	—	—
1951	4,172	1,285
1952	—	—
1953	4,817	1,394

TABLE 9
High School Principals (Cities 30,000 to 100,000)
Annual Salary Received 1904-1953

Year	Average Salary Received	Salary Deflated to "Real" Purchasing Power
1904	$1,931	$1,931
1908	—	—
1913	—	—
1916	—	—
1917	—	—
1918	—	—
1919	—	—
1920	—	—
1921	—	—
1922	—	—
1923	3,794	1,915
1924	—	—
1925	4,003	1,964
1926	—	—
1927	4,138	2,053
1928	—	—
1929	4,193	2,105
1930	—	—
1931	4,281	2,424
1932	—	—
1933	3,885	2,587
1934	—	—
1935	3,635	2,279
1936	—	—
1937	3,839	2,300
1938	—	—
1939	4,055	2,492
1940	—	—
1941	4,000	2,280
1942	—	—
1943	4,143	1,955
1944	—	—
1945	4,396	1,853
1946	—	—
1947	4,700	1,700
1948	—	—
1949	5,468	1,815
1950	—	—
1951	5,967	1,775
1952	—	—
1953	6,523	1,833

TABLE 10

High School Teachers in Small Cities (30,000 to 100,000) Annual Salary Received 1904-1953

Year	Average Salary Received	Salary Deflated to "Real" Purchasing Power
1904	$ 918	$ 918
1908	—	—
1913	1,075	936
1916	—	—
1917	—	—
1918	—	—
1919	1,263	628
1920	1,525	655
1921	—	—
1922	—	—
1923	1,917	968
1924	—	—
1925	2,000	981
1926	—	—
1927	2,060	1,022
1928	—	—
1929	2,120	1,064
1930	—	—
1931	2,111	1,195
1932	—	—
1933	1,994	1,328
1934	—	—
1935	1,834	1,150
1936	—	—
1937	1,954	1,171
1938	—	—
1939	2,029	1,246
1940	—	—
1941	2,039	1,181
1942	—	—
1943	2,215	1,059
1944	—	—
1945	2,464	1,122
1946	—	—
1947	2,774	1,022
1948	—	—
1949	3,444	1,193
1950	—	—
1951	3,782	1,179
1952	—	—
1953	4,292	1,259

TABLE 11

Elementary School Teachers in Small Cities (30,000 to 100,000) Annual Salary Received 1904-1953

Year	Average Salary Received	Salary Deflated to "Real" Purchasing Power
1904	$ 547	$ 547
1908	—	—
1913	669	582
1916	—	—
1917	—	—
1918	—	—
1919	874	435
1920	1,087	467
1921	—	—
1922	1,379	709
1923	1,466	740
1924	—	—
1925	1,528	750
1926	—	—
1927	1,565	776
1928	—	—
1929	1,607	807
1930	—	—
1931	1,609	911
1932	—	—
1933	1,526	1,016
1934	—	—
1935	1,412	885
1936	—	—
1937	1,501	899
1938	—	—
1939	1,584	972
1940	—	—
1941	1,608	932
1942	—	—
1943	1,765	855
1944	—	—
1945	1,980	920
1946	—	—
1947	2,288	869
1948	—	—
1949	2,955	1,042
1950	—	—
1951	3,231	1,030
1952	—	—
1953	3,682	1,102

TABLE 12
Elementary School Teachers in Small Towns (5,000 to 10,000) Annual Salary Received 1904-1953

Year	Average Salary Received	Income Deflated to "Real" Purchasing Power
1904	$ 446	$ 446
1908	—	—
1913	—	—
1916	—	—
1917	—	—
1918	—	—
1919	677	337
1920	—	—
1921	—	—
1922	—	—
1923	1,204	608
1924	—	—
1925	1,231	604
1926	—	—
1927	1,281	635
1928	—	—
1929	1,342	674
1930	—	—
1931	1,303	738
1932	—	—
1933	1,217	810
1934	—	—
1935	1,050	658
1936	—	—
1937	1,150	689
1938	—	—
1939	1,251	768
1940	—	—
1941	1,289	747
1942	—	—
1943	1,379	670
1944	—	—
1945	1,662	774
1946	—	—
1947	1,948	744
1948	—	—
1949	2,609	934
1950	—	—
1951	2,831	923
1952	—	—
1953	3,190	977

TABLE 13
Executive Officials, Large Railroads
Annual Salary Received 1904-1953

Year	Average Salary Received	Salary Deflated to "Real" Purchasing Power
1904	$ 2,803	$2,803
1908	3,194	3,054
1913	4,428	3,854
1916	4,508	3,561
1917	4,514	3,005
1918	4,278	2,397
1919	4,296	2,107
1920	—	—
1921	6,338	2,996
1922	6,421	3,241
1923	6,654	3,309
1924	6,827	3,415
1925	6,925	3,387
1926	7,039	3,416
1927	7,216	3,567
1928	7,322	3,663
1929	7,448	3,734
1930	7,561	3,884
1931	7,441	4,198
1932	6,673	4,134
1933	6,431	4,214
1934	6,485	4,122
1935	6,762	4,182
1936	7,027	4,298
1937	7,359	4,339
1938	7,378	4,432
1939	7,361	4,490
1940	7,390	4,443
1941	7,500	4,080
1942	7,750	3,525
1943	7,821	3,246
1944	7,882	3,201
1945	7,991	3,169
1946	8,688	3,276
1947	9,070	2,971
1948	9,671	3,060
1949	10,083	3,212
1950	10,177	3,191
1951	11,007	3,140
1952	11,265	3,057
1953	11,592	3,109

TABLE 14
Railroad Engineers
Annual Wages Received 1904-1953

Year	Average Wages Received	Wages Deflated to "Real" Purchasing Power
1904	$1,313	$1,313
1908	1,465	1,401
1913	1,661	1,446
1916	1,988	1,570
1917	2,170	1,457
1918	2,514	1,439
1919	2,828	1,407
1920	3,401	1,460
1921	2,970	1,431
1922	3,000	1,542
1923	3,064	1,547
1924	3,059	1,540
1925	3,172	1,556
1926	3,206	1,561
1927	3,191	1,583
1928	3,322	1,668
1929	3,400	1,707
1930	3,276	1,690
1931	3,194	1,809
1932	2,840	1,790
1933	2,812	1,872
1934	2,854	1,837
1935	3,156	1,979
1936	3,316	2,058
1937	3,336	1,999
1938	3,454	2,103
1939	3,530	2,181
1940	3,584	2,191
1941	3,814	2,167
1942	4,244	2,045
1943	4,456	1,963
1944	4,770	2,043
1945	4,768	2,064
1946	5,202	2,060
1947	5,253	1,815
1948	5,888	1,927
1949	6,188	2,037
1950	6,378	2,059
1951	6,486	1,917
1952	7,232	2,049
1953	7,352	2,063

TABLE 15
Railroad Conductors
Annual Wages Received 1904-1953

Year	Average Wages Received	Wages Deflated to "Real" Purchasing Power
1904	$1,116	$1,116
1908	1,282	1,226
1913	1,500	1,305
1916	1,747	1,380
1917	1,910	1,283
1918	2,274	1,302
1919	2,481	1,234
1920	3,008	1,292
1921	2,720	1,311
1922	2,733	1,405
1923	2,774	1,400
1924	2,810	1,415
1925	2,853	1,400
1926	2,879	1,402
1927	2,946	1,461
1928	2,941	1,476
1929	3,035	1,524
1930	2,963	1,528
1931	2,894	1,639
1932	2,603	1,640
1933	2,597	1,729
1934	2,647	1,703
1935	2,896	1,816
1936	3,018	1,873
1937	3,036	1,819
1938	3,138	1,916
1939	3,192	1,979
1940	3,223	1,981
1941	3,430	1,966
1942	3,860	1,883
1943	4,056	1,809
1944	4,350	1,877
1945	4,326	1,827
1946	4,791	1,911
1947	4,862	1,692
1948	5,418	1,783
1949	5,670	1,877
1950	5,830	1,894
1951	6,006	1,786
1952	6,576	1,861
1953	6,676	1,873

TABLE 16
Railroad Firemen
Annual Wages Received 1904-1953

Year	Average Wages Received	Wages Deflated to "Real" Purchasing Power
1904	$ 736	$ 736
1908	829	793
1913	954	830
1916	1,212	957
1917	1,314	882
1918	1,712	980
1919	1,997	994
1920	2,476	1,063
1921	2,148	1,035
1922	2,151	1,106
1923	2,200	1,111
1924	2,205	1,110
1925	2,308	1,132
1926	2,340	1,139
1927	2,388	1,185
1928	2,445	1,227
1929	2,506	1,258
1930	2,394	1,235
1931	2,305	1,305
1932	2,016	1,270
1933	1,912	1,273
1934	1,954	1,257
1935	2,168	1,359
1936	2,315	1,437
1937	2,355	1,411
1938	2,431	1,484
1939	2,510	1,556
1940	2,563	1,575
1941	2,790	1,604
1942	3,190	1,594
1943	3,412	1,553
1944	3,745	1,642
1945	3,726	1,599
1946	4,118	1,662
1947	4,187	1,473
1948	4,787	1,591
1949	5,081	1,696
1950	5,246	1,717
1951	5,367	1,611
1952	6,092	1,736
1953	6,180	1,745

TABLE 17
Railroad Switchtenders
Annual Wages Received 1904-1953

Year	Average Wages Received	Wages Deflated to "Real" Purchasing Power
1904	$ 583	$ 583
1908	598	572
1913	585	509
1916	756	597
1917	846	568
1918	1,151	659
1919	1,488	740
1920	1,792	770
1921	1,599	771
1922	1,521	782
1923	1,545	780
1924	1,625	818
1925	1,663	816
1926	1,694	825
1927	1,786	886
1928	1,802	905
1929	1,803	905
1930	1,792	924
1931	1,758	995
1932	1,588	1,001
1933	1,477	983
1934	1,477	950
1935	1,641	1,029
1936	1,700	1,055
1937	1,754	1,051
1938	1,866	1,139
1939	1,893	1,174
1940	1,913	1,176
1941	2,009	1,176
1942	2,253	1,163
1943	2,411	1,137
1944	2,692	1,235
1945	2,708	1,213
1946	3,102	1,290
1947	3,226	1,166
1948	3,798	1,289
1949	4,000	1,364
1950	3,986	1,337
1951	4,865	1,475
1952	4,700	1,375
1953	4,697	1,363

TABLE 18
Railroad Clerks
Annual Wages Received 1904-1953

Year	Average Wages Received	Wages Deflated to "Real" Purchasing Power
1904	$ 615	$ 615
1908	689	659
1913	711	619
1916	832	657
1917	857	576
1918	1,133	649
1919	1,254	624
1920	1,547	664
1921	1,484	715
1922	1,419	730
1923	1,415	714
1924	1,439	725
1925	1,450	711
1926	1,463	712
1927	1,494	741
1928	1,531	769
1929	1,549	778
1930	1,546	797
1931	1,531	867
1932	1,392	877
1933	1,363	907
1934	1,418	912
1935	1,552	973
1936	1,587	985
1937	1,633	978
1938	1,704	1,040
1939	1,717	1,064
1940	1,725	1,060
1941	1,822	1,066
1942	2,030	1,072
1943	2,288	1,089
1944	2,370	1,112
1945	2,376	1,089
1946	2,777	1,172
1947	2,882	1,056
1948	3,205	1,109
1949	3,336	1,159
1950	3,395	1,159
1951	3,745	1,169
1952	3,927	1,174
1953	3,984	1,180

TABLE 19
All Persons Employed by Railroads
Annual Wages Received 1904-1953

Year	Average Wages Received	Salary Deflated to "Real" Purchasing Power
1904	$ 600	$ 600
1908	667	638
1913	760	661
1916	867	685
1917	989	664
1918	1,424	815
1919	1,509	751
1920	1,817	780
1921	1,632	787
1922	1,591	818
1923	1,585	800
1924	1,570	791
1925	1,597	784
1926	1,613	785
1927	1,668	827
1928	1,699	853
1929	1,749	878
1930	1,717	886
1931	1,661	941
1932	1,461	921
1933	1,439	958
1934	1,505	968
1935	1,645	1,031
1936	1,724	1,070
1937	1,774	1,063
1938	1,849	1,129
1939	1,877	1,152
1940	1,906	1,160
1941	2,030	1,176
1942	2,303	1,185
1943	2,585	1,206
1944	2,714	1,243
1945	2,711	1,215
1946	3,055	1,273
1947	3,216	1,163
1948	3,581	1,223
1949	3,706	1,273
1950	3,789	1,278
1951	4,171	1,285
1952	4,342	1,282
1953	4,407	1,289

TABLE 20

Telephone Operators of the New York Telephone Company
Annual Wages Received (At Top Rate) 1904-1953

Year	Average Wages Received	Salary Deflated to "Real" Purchasing Power
1904	$ 468	$ 468
1908	520	497
1913	520	453
1916	624	493
1917	676	454
1918	754	432
1919	926	461
1920	1,196	514
1921	1,196	576
1922	1,196	615
1923	1,196	604
1924	1,196	602
1925	1,196	587
1926	1,196	582
1927	1,196	593
1928	1,326	666
1929	1,352	679
1930	1,404	724
1931	1,404	795
1932	1,404	885
1933	1,404	935
1934	1,456	937
1935	1,420	890
1936	1,404	872
1937	1,477	876
1938	1,508	911
1939	1,508	926
1940	1,508	918
1941	1,617	937
1942	1,768	924
1943	1,768	857
1944	1,924	914
1945	2,184	1,014
1946	2,272	989
1947	2,428	913
1948	2,600	922
1949	2,704	966
1950	2,756	967
1951	2,912	945
1952	3,068	954
1953	3,224	986

TABLE 21
Workers in the Automobile Manufacturing Industry
Annual Wages Received 1904-1953

Year	Average Wages Received	Wages Deflated to "Real" Purchasing Power
1904	$ 594	$ 594
1908	650	621
1913	804	700
1916	896	708
1917	1,060	712
1918	1,216	696
1919	1,431	712
1920	1,652	709
1921	1,498	722
1922	1,569	807
1923	1,628	822
1924	1,555	783
1925	1,652	811
1926	1,590	774
1927	1,644	815
1928	1,714	860
1929	1,813	910
1930	1,571	810
1931	1,455	824
1932	1,234	778
1933	1,170	779
1934	1,314	846
1935	1,489	934
1936	1,600	993
1937	1,672	992
1938	1,653	999
1939	1,762	1,081
1940	1,934	1,177
1941	2,243	1,300
1942	2,880	1,434
1943	2,978	1,361
1944	3,103	1,393
1945	2,968	1,311
1946	2,814	1,185
1947	3,143	1,140
1948	3,381	1,162
1949	3,608	1,243
1950	4,010	1,344
1951	4,224	1,300
1952	4,608	1,351
1953	4,947	1,428

TABLE 22
Workers in the Furniture Manufacturing Industry
Annual Wages Received 1904-1953

Year	Average Wages Received	Salary Deflated to "Real" Purchasing Power
1904	$ 452	$ 452
1908	499	477
1913	620	540
1916	610	482
1917	706	474
1918	843	483
1919	1,020	507
1920	1,261	541
1921	1,155	557
1922	1,164	598
1923	1,217	614
1924	1,222	615
1925	1,245	611
1926	1,284	625
1927	1,278	634
1928	1,267	636
1929	1,398	702
1930	1,310	676
1931	1,196	677
1932	962	606
1933	900	599
1934	948	610
1935	988	619
1936	1,074	667
1937	1,123	666
1938	1,102	666
1939	1,138	699
1940	1,158	704
1941	1,304	755
1942	1,514	792
1943	1,743	845
1944	1,892	899
1945	1,988	923
1946	2,187	956
1947	2,395	903
1948	2,777	979
1949	2,837	1,007
1950	3,011	1,043
1951	3,242	1,033
1952	3,434	1,047
1953	3,570	1,073

TABLE 23
Workers in the Electrical Machinery Manufacturing Industry
Annual Wages Received 1904-1953

Year	Average Wages Received	Salary Deflated to "Real" Purchasing Power
1904	$ 527	$ 527
1908	550	526
1913	642	559
1916	705	557
1917	782	525
1918	992	568
1919	1,121	558
1920	1,335	573
1921	1,205	581
1922	1,143	588
1923	1,300	656
1924	1,339	674
1925	1,350	662
1926	1,352	658
1927	1,365	677
1928	1,383	694
1929	1,655	831
1930	1,658	855
1931	1,461	827
1932	1,182	745
1933	1,203	801
1934	1,282	825
1935	1,364	855
1936	1,478	917
1937	1,616	959
1938	1,527	923
1939	1,601	983
1940	1,688	1,027
1941	1,919	1,112
1942	2,287	1,177
1943	2,466	1,159
1944	2,578	1,191
1945	2,584	1,167
1946	2,615	1,113
1947	2,876	1,054
1948	3,153	1,093
1949	3,250	1,133
1950	3,370	1,151
1951	3,714	1,160
1952	3,959	1,182
1953	4,133	1,218

TABLE 24
Workers in the Tobacco Manufacturing Industry
Annual Wages Received 1904-1953

Year	Average Wages Received	Wages Deflated to "Real" Purchasing Power
1904	$ 413	$ 413
1908	440	421
1913	453	394
1916	479	378
1917	540	363
1918	621	355
1919	802	399
1920	937	402
1921	811	391
1922	798	410
1923	823	415
1924	852	429
1925	849	417
1926	863	420
1927	832	413
1928	818	411
1929	979	491
1930	985	508
1931	908	514
1932	787	496
1933	725	483
1934	750	483
1935	778	488
1936	817	507
1937	883	524
1938	870	526
1939	916	562
1940	1,000	608
1941	1,117	647
1942	1,240	649
1943	1,431	695
1944	1,580	752
1945	1,676	780
1946	1,779	777
1947	1,950	744
1948	2,040	723
1949	2,089	748
1950	2,258	797
1951	2,447	807
1952	2,592	828
1953	2,709	856

TABLE 25
Workers in the Bituminous Coal Mining Industry
Annual Wages Received 1904-1953

Year	Average Wages Received	Salary Deflated to "Real" Purchasing Power
1904	$ 470	$ 470
1908	487	466
1913	631	549
1916	750	592
1917	976	655
1918	1,211	693
1919	1,097	546
1920	1,386	595
1921	1,013	488
1922	954	490
1923	1,246	629
1924	1,120	564
1925	1,141	560
1926	1,247	607
1927	1,099	545
1928	1,152	578
1929	1,293	649
1930	1,119	577
1931	909	515
1932	723	456
1933	748	498
1934	900	579
1935	957	600
1936	1,103	685
1937	1,170	694
1938	1,050	635
1939	1,197	735
1940	1,235	752
1941	1,500	869
1942	1,715	897
1943	2,115	1,017
1944	2,535	1,175
1945	2,629	1,184
1946	2,724	1,153
1947	3,212	1,162
1948	3,383	1,163
1949	2,930	1,035
1950	3,268	1,120
1951	3,831	1,192
1952	3,780	1,136
1953	4,198	1,235

TABLE 26
Workers in the Stone, Clay and Glass Manufacturing Industry Annual Wages Received 1904-1953

Year	Average Wages Received	Salary Deflated to "Real" Purchasing Power
1904	$ 527	$ 527
1908	528	505
1913	599	521
1916	590	466
1917	693	465
1918	891	510
1919	1,085	540
1920	1,360	584
1921	1,206	581
1922	1,154	593
1923	1,274	643
1924	1,307	658
1925	1,310	643
1926	1,329	647
1927	1,309	649
1928	1,331	668
1929	1,557	782
1930	1,525	786
1931	1,386	785
1932	1,167	735
1933	1,071	713
1934	1,088	700
1935	1,171	734
1936	1,262	783
1937	1,357	805
1938	1,303	788
1939	1,359	834
1940	1,393	848
1941	1,554	900
1942	1,771	926
1943	2,024	979
1944	2,174	1,032
1945	2,249	1,042
1946	2,380	1,028
1947	2,672	990
1948	2,925	1,024
1949	3,008	1,059
1950	3,239	1,111
1951	3,595	1,128
1952	3,702	1,116
1953	3,956	1,172

TABLE 27
All Workers in Manufacturing Industries
Annual Wages Received 1904-1953

Year	Average Wages Received	Salary Deflated to "Real" Purchasing Power
1904	$ 477	$ 477
1908	475	454
1913	578	503
1916	651	514
1917	774	520
1918	980	561
1919	1,158	576
1920	1,358	583
1921	1,180	569
1922	1,149	591
1923	1,254	633
1924	1,240	624
1925	1,280	628
1926	1,309	637
1927	1,299	644
1928	1,325	665
1929	1,543	775
1930	1,488	767
1931	1,369	775
1932	1,150	725
1933	1,086	723
1934	1,153	742
1935	1,216	762
1936	1,287	799
1937	1,376	816
1938	1,296	783
1939	1,363	836
1940	1,432	872
1941	1,653	957
1942	2,023	1,058
1943	2,349	1,113
1944	2,517	1,168
1945	2,517	1,142
1946	2,517	1,078
1947	2,793	1,028
1948	3,040	1,058
1949	3,092	1,084
1950	3,300	1,130
1951	3,612	1,132
1952	3,834	1,150
1953	4,051	1,197

TABLE 28
Physicians
Annual Net Income 1929-1953

Year	Average Net Income	Income Deflated to "Real" Purchasing Power
1904	—	—
1908	—	—
1913	—	—
1916	—	—
1917	—	—
1918	—	—
1919	—	—
1920	—	—
1921	—	—
1922	—	—
1923	—	—
1924	—	—
1925	—	—
1926	—	—
1927	—	—
1928	—	—
1929	$ 5,224	$2,622
1930	—	—
1931	4,178	2,366
1932	—	—
1933	2,948	1,963
1934	—	—
1935	3,695	2,317
1936	—	—
1937	4,285	2,567
1938	—	—
1939	4,229	2,622
1940	—	—
1941	5,047	2,820
1942	—	—
1943	8,370	3,447
1944	—	—
1945	10,975	4,182
1946	—	—
1947	10,726	3,444
1948	—	—
1949	—	—
1950	12,324	3,804
1951	—	—
1952	—	—
1953	15,000	3,888

Note: Figures are deflated back to 1904 levels of purchasing power in this table for convenience in comparison with other figures in this report.

TABLE 29
Dentists
Annual Net Income 1929-1953

Year	Average Net Income	Income Deflated to "Real" Purchasing Power
1904	—	—
1908	—	—
1913	—	—
1916	—	—
1917	—	—
1918	—	—
1919	—	—
1920	—	—
1921	—	—
1922	—	—
1923	—	—
1924	—	—
1925	—	—
1926	—	—
1927	—	—
1928	—	—
1929	$4,267	$2,142
1930	—	—
1931	3,422	1,938
1932	—	—
1933	2,188	1,457
1934	—	—
1935	2,485	1,558
1936	—	—
1937	2,883	1,727
1938	—	—
1939	3,096	1,919
1940	—	—
1941	3,782	2,152
1942	—	—
1943	5,715	2,456
1944	—	—
1945	6,922	2,792
1946	—	—
1947	6,610	2,241
1948	—	—
1949	—	—
1950	7,436	2,386
1951	—	—
1952	—	—
1953	8,500	2,350

Note: Figures are deflated back to 1904 levels of purchasing power in this table for convenience in comparison with other figures in this report.

APPENDIX B — STATISTICAL NOTES

(I) Sources and Bases of Figures

All figures on annual wages and salaries in this report are derived from tabulations, calculations or estimates made by Government agencies, trade associations or private research organizations or universities. No new field studies of wages and salaries were undertaken. Accordingly, data are available only for those sections of the economy for which specific tabulations or estimates of wages and salaries on an annual basis have already been made.

1. *Presidents of Large Universities (average salaries)*

The figures used in this report are for land grant colleges and universities only. They are on a "cash" basis, that is, they do not include the value of perquisites such as a dwelling, an automobile, entertainment or expense accounts, contributions to pension funds, and health or other benefit programs. Some perquisites and retirement or benefit plans existed throughout the period studied in some universities, but not in others. The value has grown undoubtedly in recent years.

The figures were derived as follows:
1904:
Our estimates, based on an analysis of salaries listed in *Statistics of State Universities and Other Institutions of Higher Education*, Bureau of Education, Department of Interior, Bulletin No. 8, 1908.

1922-52:
Faculty Salaries in Land Grant Colleges and State Universities, Office of Education, United States Department of Health, Education and Welfare, Circular No. 358. United States Government Printing Office, Washington, D.C., 1953. The Office of Education

survey of faculty salaries in colleges and universities was not made on a regular bi-annual basis; figures are missing, therefore, for some years. Where necessary for our analysis, some interpolations have been made.

1953:

Extrapolated from 1952 figures after an analysis of changes reported for some of the larger institutions for which data were obtained.

2. *Professors, Associate Professors, Assistant Professors and Instructors in Land Grant Colleges and State Universities (average salaries)*

The figures shown in our tables represent medians of salaries paid in land grant colleges and universities. They do not include perquisites, if any, or the value of any retirement plans or benefit programs. They exclude compensation for administrative duties (such as amounts paid for acting as a dean, or the head of a department) and amounts paid for employment in laboratories or government projects, which are outside of the regular academic duties; also excluded are supplementary sources of income such as writing, lecturing and consulting.

The figures are derived from the following sources:

1904:

Our estimates, extrapolated back from the 1908 figures, after examining various compilations by the Carnegie Foundation published in annual reports issued between 1906 and 1908.

1908-1942:

Stigler, George J., *Employment and Compensation in Education* (Occasional Paper No. 33, National Bureau of Economic Research, New York 1950, p. 42). The figures are based partly on surveys by the Office of Education and by Viva Boothe, whose report *Salaries and Cost of Living in Twenty-Seven State Universities and Colleges, 1930-32* was published by the Ohio State University Press in 1932. Stigler provides (p. 72) a description of the figures used both by him and by Miss Boothe. From his study he concludes that the information for the earlier and the later years is not strictly comparable, but he feels that the figures portray reliably the broader movements of salaries over the years. Stigler's study indicates that average salaries for each rank in the faculty are more useful than averages for faculty members together because of changes in the relative number of people in the various ranks; and that for a large part of the period studied, at any rate, the trend of salaries in all colleges and universities as a whole is portrayed by the trend in large public institutions.

1943-49:

Our estimates interpolated between the 1942 and 1950 data. Surveys of faculty salaries were not made by the Office of Education during this period.

1950-52:

Faculty Salaries in Land Grant Colleges and State Universities, Office of Education, United States Department of Health, Education and Welfare, Circular No. 358, United States Government Printing Office, Washington, D.C., 1953. The figures used are those reported for a nine month basis for 52 land grant universities and colleges (figures for 17 land grant institutions for negroes are excluded). Stigler's analysis indicated that figures on this basis are comparable to earlier figures appearing in his report and Boothe's report.

1953:

Our estimates extrapolated from 1952 data.

3. *Teachers and Principals in the Public Schools*

The figures represent medians of salaries paid in public schools and are derived primarily from tabulations made by the National

Education Association over the years. The particular sources used in preparing the tables in the report were the following:

1904:

Report of the Committee on Salaries, Tenure and Pensions of Public School Teachers in the United States published by the National Education Association, Washington, D.C., 1905. We tabulated and analyzed the detailed figures in this report and made estimates for population classifications comparable to those used by the National Education Association in its tabulations in subsequent years.

1913-53:

Salaries and Salary Schedule of Urban School Employees, 1952-53, National Education Association, Washington, D.C., April, 1953, and prior comparable reports back to 1923. The report for 1923 entitled, *Teacher's Salaries and Salary Trends in 1923* carried the figures back to 1913. Some of the figures have been revised over the years, and in a few cases special tabulations were made by the N.E.A.

4. *Railroad Employees*

The figures are for Class I railroads only, and are based originally on tabulations made by the Interstate Commerce Commission of the total employment in various employee classifications, and the total payroll in those classifications. The classifications varied slightly over the years, but not enough to impair comparisons. The figures for executive officials include main office executives, general officials and assistants; they exclude division officials. The figures for engineers, firemen, and conductors are averages of both passenger and freight trains.

The figures in our tables are derived specifically from the following sources:

1904-13:

Data from the Interstate Commerce Commission published by the United States Bureau of the Census in the *Statistical Abstract of the United States, 1916* showed the total number of employees and the aggregate wages for various employee classifications. We calculated the average wages for our table.

1914-52:

Data from the Interstate Commerce Commission were tabulated by the Association of American Railroads, and published in the report entitled, *Railroad Wages and Labor Relations, 1900-52,* an historical survey and summary of results by Harry E. Jones, Chairman, Executive Committee, Bureau of Information of the Eastern Railways, New York, November, 1953.

1953:

Preliminary figures from Interstate Commerce Commission tabulations were provided by the Bureau of Railway Economics, Association of American Railways, Washington, D.C.

5. *Telephone Operators*

The figures represent the top of the salary scale according to the wage agreement schedules of the New York Telephone Company, and were obtained directly from the company. The figures are higher than average salaries of telephone operators, but the trend over the years is likely to be the same as for the average. The annual figure represents 52 times the weekly rate. Telephone operators received paid vacations, sick leave, etc. so this is considered a reasonable multiplication. No allowance is made for unemployment, if any, during the period. This would affect the figures for particular years, but would not be a significant factor in the analysis of the long term trend.

6. *Employees in the Automobile Manufacturing, Furniture Manufacturing, Electrical Machinery Manufacturing, Tobacco Manufacturing, Stone, Clay and Glass Manufacturing and the Bituminous Coal Mining Industries.*

The figures shown in our tables are averages for all people employed in the various industries. Figures for years at the beginning of the series and at the end of the series may not be completely comparable because of differences in the technique of compilation developed over the years, but the differences are not great enough to affect the trend. The limitations of this study made it necessary to restrict the number of industries for which data could be tabulated. The particular industries selected were picked so as to provide variety for the comparisons. No attempt was made to be completely inclusive.

The source of the figures was as follows:

1904-26:

Douglas, Paul H., *Real Wages in the United States, 1890-1926,* Chicago, 1930. This study contains a considerable amount of detail on wages and salaries in various industries. The figures differ slightly from the computations for subsequent periods made by the Department of Commerce, but the differences are not great enough to impair an analysis of wage movements over the years.

1927-28:

Douglas and Jennison, *The Movement of Money and Real Earnings, 1926-28,* Chicago, University of Chicago Press, 1930. This study carried the figures forward for two years.

1929-53:

National Income and Product 1929-53, National Income Supplement to the Survey of Current Business, Department of Commerce, July, 1954, U. S. Government Printing Office, Washington, D.C. Figures used are average annual earnings per full-time employee. The basic data were obtained by the Department of Commerce for the national income survey; annual earnings were arrived at by dividing total wages and salaries in each industry by the number of full-time-equivalent employees. Full-time-equivalent employment comprises man-years of full-time employment plus the equivalent in work performed by part-time workers.

7. Physicians and Dentists

1929:50:

Survey of Current Business, United States Department of Commerce, Office of Business Economics. Various issues 1949-52, U.S. Government Printing Office, Washington, D.C. The figures came from special surveys by the Department and represent average net professional income of non-salaried practitioners after professional expenses have been paid and before payment of income taxes.

1953:

Our estimates based on a discussion with the Department of Commerce of the amounts that would be implied in the regular national income survey.

8. Specific Salaries, 1908

The figures in Tables H, I and J on salaries paid in specific positions in 1908 were obtained as follows:

(a) President's salary and salary of highest paid professors at University of Chicago: by correspondence with Dr. Lawrence A. Kimpton, Chancellor, University of Chicago, April 1955.

(b) President's salary and salary of highest paid professors at other universities: *Statistics of State Universities and Other Institutions of Higher Education,* Bureau of Education, Department of Interior, Bulletin No. 8, 1908.

(c) Superintendent of Schools, City of New York: from the Office of the Superintendent, by telephone, March 1955.

(d) Commissioner of Education, State of New York: *Teachers Salaries and Salary Trends in 1923,* National Education Association of the United States, Washington, D.C. 1923. Historical tables in this report include data on salaries of top education officials in each State in 1908.

(II) Deflation of Salaries and Wages to "Real" Purchasing Power

The salary and wage figures in this report have been deflated back to 1904 levels of "real" purchasing power by deducting the amount of Federal income taxes and social security taxes paid and then applying the change in the level of prices shown by the Consumers Price Index of the Bureau of Labor Statistics. The total of salary or wages minus Federal taxes provides a figure described as "Net Spendable Earnings." The concept and its use are described by the Department of Labor in the January 1953 issue of the *Monthly Labor Review,* as follows:

"Spendable earnings are obtained by deducting from gross earnings the Federal social security and income taxes for which a worker with no dependents and a worker with three dependents is liable.

"Changes in net spendable weekly earnings indicate changes in the ability of the employed factory worker to purchase goods and services. The sellers of goods and services can use this information with other data to evaluate the extent of changes in the market for their products. In addition, the measurement of changes in ability to buy throws light on the extent to which the economy provides the factory worker and his family the opportunity to enhance their level of living.

"Until 1939, gross earnings of most factory workers were not affected by Federal income taxes, and the social security deductions were only one percent. At that time, however, the defense buildup brought about the extension of Federal income taxes to wage levels that included practically all factory workers. As income tax payments grew and were regularly deducted from the worker's pay, the gross earnings data bore less and less relationship to what he had left for spending out of his weekly pay. Thus, it became desirable to measure spendable earnings.

"It was further recognized that, as a measure of the worker's ability to buy goods and services, net spendable earnings were influenced by changes in the dollar's purchasing power. To take account of these changes, the two computed net spendable series were adjusted by the Consumer Price Index."

Tax Calculations

For the period 1939-53, the Federal income taxes due from workers in the middle and lower income brackets were computed by the application of formulas worked out by the Bureau of Labor Statistics in connection with its computations of net spendable earnings of factory workers. For amounts of income in excess of the brackets covered by the BLS formulas, the following procedure was used:

(a) Up to 1950: taxes were estimated by interpolating between published estimates of taxes due at various income levels. These have been worked out by the U.S. Treasury Department from time to time and were summarized in tables in the *Annual Report of the Secretary of the Treasury on the State of the Finances for the Fiscal Year 1950*, p. 245, U.S. Government Printing Office, Washington, D.C.

(b) For 1951-1953: actual tax computations were made using the schedules provided by the Bureau of Internal Revenue.

In all cases, it was assumed that the standard deduction for expenses applied. All school employees were considered exempt from the Federal income tax until 1939, and subject to this tax and to social security taxes thereafter. Railroad employees, physicians and dentists were considered exempt from social security taxes throughout the period. The value of perquisites and privileges (free transportation, health plans, meals, etc.) was excluded from the consideration in all cases. Tax calculations were made for a married person with two children. Other assumptions as to deductions, exemptions, and type of income, could have been made, but the figures arrived at would not have changed the conclusions in this report.

Cost of Living

After the Federal income taxes (and social security, where applicable) had been computed and deducted from the amount of wages or salaries, the remainder was deflated to the 1904 level of purchasing power by the application of a change in prices factor based upon the Consumer Price Index published by the Bureau of Labor Statistics. The BLS Index, technically called the "Index of Change in Prices of Goods and Services Purchased by City Wage Earner and Clerical Worker Families to Maintain Their Level of Living," is likely to be satisfactory, generally, to adjust the expenditures by the various categories of wage earners and teachers studied in this report. It is recognized, however, that the BLS Consumer Price Index does not apply precisely to all consumers, to all income levels, or to all parts of the country. The differences that would occur by using other cost of living factors to deflate the wage and salary figures to real purchasing power are small, however, and would not affect the conclusions in this report.

The Bureau of Labor Statistics uses 1947-49 as the base for its index and the figure of 100 represents a weighted average index of the prices of certain commodities in these years. In this study the price index is converted to a basis of 1904 = 100. The BLS figures were used as the basis back to 1913 and figures from the Federal Reserve Bank of New York were then used as the basis back to 1904. A table follows, showing the figures reported by the various agencies and the converted figures.

CONSUMER PRICE INDEX
1904-1953

Year	BLS Index 1947-9 = 100	BLS Index Converted 1904 = 100
1904	36.8	100.0
1905	36.8	100.0
1906	38.1	103.5
1907	40.2	109.2
1908	38.5	104.6
1909	38.5	104.6
1910	40.6	110.3
1911	40.6	110.3
1912	43.1	117.1
1913	42.3	114.9
1914	42.9	116.5
1915	43.4	117.9
1916	46.6	126.6
1917	54.8	148.9
1918	64.3	174.7
1919	74.0	201.0
1920	85.7	232.9
1921	76.4	207.5
1922	71.6	194.5
1923	72.9	198.1
1924	73.1	198.6
1925	75.0	203.8
1926	75.6	205.4
1927	74.2	201.6
1928	73.3	199.2

CONSUMER PRICE INDEX
1904-1953

Year	BLS Index 1947-9 = 100	BLS Index Converted 1904 = 100
1929	73.3	199.2
1930	71.4	193.9
1931	65.0	176.6
1932	58.4	158.7
1933	55.3	150.2
1934	57.2	155.4
1935	58.7	159.5
1936	59.3	161.1
1937	61.4	166.9
1938	60.3	163.8
1939	59.4	161.3
1940	59.9	162.7
1941	62.9	170.9
1942	69.7	189.3
1943	74.0	201.0
1944	75.2	204.3
1945	76.9	208.9
1946	83.4	226.5
1947	95.5	259.4
1948	102.8	279.2
1949	101.8	276.6
1950	102.8	279.2
1951	110.0	298.8
1952	113.5	308.4
1953	114.4	310.8

Note: Figures for 1913-1953 from Bureau of Labor Statistics. Figures for 1904-1913 from Federal Reserve Bank of New York and converted to the 1947-1949 basis.

MANUFACTURED IN THE UNITED STATES OF AMERICA